SECOND GENERATION WEALTH

WHAT DO YOU WANT FOR YOUR KIDS?

J. TED OAKLEY

RIVER GROVE
BOOKS

Published by River Grove Books
Austin, TX
www.rivergrovebooks.com

Distributed by River Grove Books

Design and composition by Greenleaf Book Group and Mimi Bark
Cover design by Brad Deutser

Publisher's Cataloging-in-Publication data is available.

Print ISBN: 9781966629160

eBook ISBN: 9781966629184

First Edition

At Oxbow Advisors, we're not Wall Street. We are an Austin, Texas-based wealth management company specializing in the needs of families with significant wealth—many of them just this side of liquidity events, such as selling a business or inheriting assets.

Unlike many of the investment firms at your door, we're not paid to sell you any product, any portfolio, anything. Instead, as independent advisors, we assess all options in search of the best quality investments to fit your needs and those of your family.

What we do is simple, but hard to find in today's investment world: We protect the wealth you've worked hard to create. You tell us what you need to achieve financially—for yourself and for your family—and our job is to help you get there.

Oxbow Advisors
OxbowAdvisors.com
512-386-1088

CONTENTS

Introduction

RAISING GROUNDED CHILDREN IN A WORLD OF WEALTH

C arl Sandburg wrote that money is "power, freedom, a cushion, the root of all evil, the sum of blessings." That wide-ranging assessment hints at the complexity of wealth, and nowhere does the topic of money get more complicated than in matters of inheritance. Your wealth can be of great benefit to your children and grandchildren, giving them the advantages of excellent educations, homes in desirable neighborhoods, and financial safety nets. But it can also undermine their confidence, be an impediment to their independence, and drive wedges between them and their siblings, extended family, and friends. You don't hold all the power in deciding which way this goes, but your actions can help ensure the money becomes a force for good in your kids' lives instead of the seed of hardship and unhappiness.

In four decades of counseling families in the management of significant wealth, I can tell you the impact the money will have on the kids eventually becomes the number one concern of most first-generation fortune-makers and second-gen inheritors who keep the family fortune intact. Consider some common scenarios:

- Some parents reflexively rely on their wealth to curb their kids—their behaviors, interests, educations, careers, and even their choice of life partners. Most find that using money to manage personality is a losing proposition. In Chapters 1 and 2, we'll talk about creating a healthy respect for wealth without letting it become a much resented implement of control in your kids' lives.

- Most parents imagine their wealth will make life easy for their kids across the board. The matriarch and patriarch may have struggled and suffered building their businesses, and they want nothing more than to spare their children hardships like those they endured. In Chapter 3, you'll read about why I counsel these parents to be careful what they wish for. Struggle and self-esteem are usually two sides of the same coin—and without one, your kids are likely to lack the other. In Chapter 4, we'll talk about how the precedents you set will help your heirs develop healthy—or destructive—relationships with family wealth.

- Some parents have an inkling the money could cause trouble, and they seek advice on how and when to begin teaching the heirs what the family has, what they will one day inherit, and how to put the money in the context of full, productive lives. In Chapters 5 and 6, we'll delve into these topics in detail (and I'll explain why I dislike the phrase "family governance" and advise against plans that bring teens and very young adults to the table to strategize about family investments and estate plans).

- No matter how parents approach educating and distributing wealth, one factor most fail to consider are people who aren't in the family when they make their plans. In-laws, hanger-on friends, and distant relatives can derail succession plans with their presence and their preferences. Equally important, many first-generation wealth earners don't do enough to ensure resources make it to Gen Three—the grandchildren. In Chapter 7, I'll share cautions and strategies for ensuring you're not overlooking these key players.

- Finally, in Chapter 8, we'll talk about the one cardinal rule every family must consider and respect—especially if they want their kids to still be on speaking terms after they're gone.

At Oxbow, the wealth advisory firm I founded to help guide families to long-term, multi-generational financial health, we've had the privilege of witnessing thousands of legacy stories. The best of those end with well-adjusted, happy second- and third-generation heirs who see the well of family wealth as what it should be: a much-appreciated and wisely implemented resource.

The worst of them, however, end up with heirs who seem to be poisoned by that same well.

The chapters ahead will share experiences from both kinds of families, and they'll offer guidance on how you can gift a portion of your hard-earned wealth without compromising your heirs' productivity and sense of self-worth.

Chapter 1

WHAT DO YOU WANT FOR FUTURE GENERATIONS?

When you think about what you most want for your children and grandchildren, I bet your first concern isn't whether they'll be rich. Instead, it's whether they'll be safe, whether they'll be happy, and whether they'll be healthy. In addition to those goals for your offspring, consider these: You want them to be self-assured, independent, active, and fulfilled.

What do all these attributes have in common? Money can only take you so far. In fact, when handled incorrectly, family wealth can sometimes stand like so much brick wall between your kids and their best lives as adults. It happens all too often. In my decades in financial advising, I've had countless parents who seem to have everything come into my office, slump in a chair, and say, "We don't know what to do about the kids." Sometimes they say it in confusion, sometimes in frustration, and sometimes with tears in their eyes. All of them want to see their children—regardless of their age or stage of life—living full, healthy, happy lives. They want to help, but they don't want to create or worsen their kids' insecurities or their dependence.

I've seen families handle the transition of wealth in just about every way you can imagine. In the best cases, they've done it with grace, fairness, and a healthy dose of restraint. In the worst cases, they've demonstrated all the ways the transition of wealth can go wrong, including:

- Parents who treat their kids like royal princes and princesses, spoiling them before they ever have a chance to know what it's like to want, wait, or earn.

- Parents who expect the kids to follow in their footsteps—including trying to fulfill dreams they couldn't achieve in their own youth.

- Parents wielding wealth like carrot, stick, or both—compelling kids to do their bidding and inextricably tangling their power with their affection.

- Parents who become petty, marching to their attorneys every year to cut one or another heir out of their will for some perceived slight or shortcoming.

- Parents who deliberately or inadvertently pit siblings against one another, setting up lifetimes of resentment and distance.

- Parents who use the money to keep the "kids" tied to them, even after those kids turn 20, 40, or even 60 years old.

Trust me when I say you don't want to join ranks with any of these misguided patriarchs and matriarchs. There are better ways to plan your legacy. You can prepare your offspring to walk their own paths with some strength, empathy, and joy. Ultimately, you cannot dictate which directions they will take—but if you manage the variables that are within your control, you can know you've done your part to help them build meaningful, prosperous lives.

The ultimate job of a wealthy parent isn't to prop your kids up with the lifetime's worth of wealth and power you've amassed. It is helping them learn to stand alone—something they must be able to do with or without the money.

THE TRUTH ABOUT LEGACY

For the small percentage of families who manage to build substantial wealth, "legacy" can feel like a loaded term. There's an entire industry of specialists billed as *legacy advisors* and *legacy planners*, but the primary role they play is in helping you figure out how and when to give the kids your money.

I implore you to think about your legacy in terms of something bigger. The word has many shades of meaning, and most of them go beyond anything that can be given away. Your legacy is your fortune, sure. But it is equally the lasting sense of who you were and how you made people feel in your lifetime. You can, for example, leave a legacy of hard work and honest effort, a legacy of genius and creativity, a legacy of love and laughter, or a legacy of strength and character.

Of course, you can just as easily leave a legacy of pain, anger, bitterness, or manipulation.

Nobody wants the latter, and that's why you owe it to yourself and your family to ensure the legacy you're building is one of personal character and connection, just as much as it is one of wealth. The legacy you leave for the wider world matters a great deal, but in the end, the legacy you leave your family matters more. They'll either pick it up and carry it forward with pride and affection, or they'll spend their lives trying to get free of it.

Focus on the people and the values first (more about this in the chapters to come), and you'll be heading in the right direction.

A STORY OF MORE THAN MONEY

Consider the story of a young John Rockefeller. For six weeks in the summer of 1855, 16-year-old John walked the streets of Cleveland, knocking on doors at company after company, asking for a job. He pounded the pavement six days a week, sweating through his dark suit and getting blisters on his feet. Finally, on September 26, he heard the words he'd been waiting for from the owner of a produce shipper who needed a bookkeeper: "We'll give you a chance."

Rockefeller never forgot that day or the mixture of excitement, relief, and gratitude he felt when he finally landed a job. For the rest of his life, he would celebrate September 26 as Job Day.

More than 80 years later, Rockefeller would pass away and leave an estate encompassing one of the greatest fortunes in American history. At least six generations have benefited from Rockefeller's financial achievements. The family has deftly managed to seed generation after generation with its wealth.

Rockefeller's legacy is a complicated one, much dependent on who is telling the tale, but that story of his first job, of how much it meant to him, and of what it would ultimately help him build for his heirs—that story lives on in the family and in the world. It's become emblematic of self-reliance, determination, and appreciation. The man built an empire from the ground up, but he remained grateful for that first opportunity.

What stories will your kids tell about you, about how you built your wealth, and about how you used it? Those stories will help define how they remember you and what they tell your grandchildren and great-grandchildren about you. They'll also help determine how they handle the fortune you leave them. The money without the story is an incomplete legacy, and a potentially damaging one. Anyone in line to inherit wealth needs context to appreciate it, protect it, and keep it from becoming the central fact of their lives.

Whether you're looking ahead for small children, teens, young adults, middle-aged heirs, grandchildren, or other family members who are precious to you, stay mindful that the fortune you leave behind and the legacy of how they remember you and your influence on their lives can't be separated. Don't neglect one side of this equation in service of the other.

DRAFT A LASTING CONNECTION

Showing your kids your values through your actions is your best legacy tool (see Chapter 4 for more about this). Here's another one I've come to regard as highly valuable for wealth creators: Rather than counting on oral history alone to share your experience, consider making your story available for them for the long term. Sit down at your desk or contract a writer to help you write a short biography. You don't want to leave them a *War and Peace*-sized volume, but rather a collection of favorite tales from your childhood, stories of hardship and overcoming, stories of smart business decisions, stories of kindnesses or strengths the kids might not have seen, and stories of how your partner's and kids' lives changed yours.

Creating a written history of who you and your spouse are and how hard it was to get to your position—about the long days, the lean years, and about what your achievement truly means to you—may be the best way to help your grandchildren and future great-grandchildren know about your character and the origins of the family fortune. The point in these tales is to share not just your accomplishments, but your struggles. Writing them down (or recording them, if you prefer) will create a lasting connection for your family that reminds them not just of you, but that life is a series of obstacles and achievements, and our purpose is to keep moving forward.

OXBOW NOTE:

If you are a first-generation wealth earner who recently sold your company, this is a critical time in your financial life and an area of specialization for us at Oxbow Advisors. For free copies of more of our books about this make-or-break time, contact us at OxbowAdvisors.com.

Chapter 2

HOW DO YOU VIEW
YOUR OFFSPRING?

Sooner or later, we all learn the same lesson about parenting: that our children are separate, independent human beings from us. They must make their own decisions, stand on their own feet, and find their own happiness. Plenty of parents from all rungs on the wealth ladder struggle with this truth. It can be especially difficult to accept, though, for parents who've accomplished great things—like those who have built their own businesses and accumulated significant wealth. There's a good chance that if you've hit those marks, you're exceptional in some way. Maybe you're highly intelligent or innovative. Maybe you're a natural leader. Maybe you have a gift for reading people and recognizing their needs. Maybe you've always been the hardest worker, lapping your competition through your effort. Maybe—probably—you're also a bit lucky. You may have a mix of these traits, and you've likely earned a great deal of respect and admiration along your path to success.

It's no wonder it's tough to accept that even with all you've accomplished, your personality and priorities will not automatically spill over to your children. Truth is, they may gravitate in another direction, or, they may reject what you consider your best and strongest qualities altogether. This can be hard to swallow, but still a good thing. Consider the alternative: heirs who are content to ride their parents' coattails and live in their shadows all their lives.

Which is worse? As someone who's seen heirs of all ages still tied to the family apron strings, still lacking any confidence or conviction, I'd wager it's the coattail kids who miss out on the most.

With this in mind, take a wide view as you plan your legacy. Look at your kids, and take them as separate individuals with priorities, feelings, and concerns of their own.

MEASURE-UP PARENTS

I have seen far too many families torn apart by disagreements about where a kid will go to college, what degree they're going to get, or Dad laying down the law about their lifestyle, choice of friends, or career objectives. These are all losing battles, because if your child goes their own way and you refuse to acknowledge their independence, your connection will suffer. And if you win these battles and mold your kids to fit your own desires, they'll soon resent you for it.

Despite the negative outcomes, I see a lot of these "measure-up" parents. They may have been super successful at creating a company, at leading a team, at making a lot of money. They may have built their own boat, kicked their addiction, or started a foundation. These are all awesome accomplishments, but it cheapens them when the parent tells the kids, "By the time I was your age, I'd made $10 million." Or, "I quit alcohol 25 years ago, and you need to just stop like I did." Or, "I've helped a thousand people get their groceries or pay their power bills this year—what have you done?"

The motivations behind these statements are often more pure than they sound. Parents do want their kids to be financially secure, sober, and generous. We get frustrated when they're not. Wealthy clients carry an extra level of angst over common struggles and failings of youth because they're always on the cusp of swooping in to take off the pressure and solve the kids' problems for them.

Sadly, implying (or outright stating) that the children or grandchildren don't measure up is almost always a bad play, because it creates expectations for the kids that keep them in the "never enough" column. No matter what they do—even if they build their own fortunes and win their own battles—they'll never be able to live up to the standard of being just like you or everything you think they can be. I see this far too often, and it looks like a heartbreak coming every time.

Rather than compare your success to their success, consider that maturity takes time. So does self-confidence. Remember that you had ups and downs, that you may not have been successful at a young age, and that every life has a long learning curve. Give your children and grandchildren time and space to figure out their own roles. Let them learn. Be there and believe in them, but don't try to dictate their lessons or the timetables on which they learn them. If they're out in the world striving and accomplishing and sometimes failing on their own terms, they'll find their way to growth.

No matter how far apart your assessment of success and that of your heirs are, keep in mind that it really doesn't matter whether they can make their own multi-million dollar fortune. You've already done that. In the long run, you plan to leave them with plenty of money. What they actually need is to know, deep down, that they can survive and achieve on their own.

SKIP THE POWER PLAYS

One of the worst habits wealthy individuals can pick up is conflating money with absolute power. Yes, money and power overlap all over the place, but when it comes to family dynamics, it's best to create separation between them. I see far too many parents who wield their financial advantages like blunt instruments, pushing and pulling kids in the directions they want them to take. Stop and think hard before you engage in this behavior. Do you want your kids to grow into adults who simply do as they're told? Who bow to money above all else? Who are always looking to someone to tell them what to do or make their path easier for them?

Of course not. We want kids who are strong and upright, and helping them get that way means choosing not to bend them to your will using your wealth. Whether you've got $50 million in the bank or $500 million, using it to force anything on your kids may either make them permanently dependent or push them out of your orbit altogether.

Examples of this abound: the son forced to attend Dad's alma mater; the daughter shackled to a family firm career before she's even started college; the heir who's told the life partner they've chosen won't be accepted by the family.

MANIPULATION CAN GO BOTH WAYS

I advise parents to be mindful that laying off power plays also means not falling for them. Some children of wealthy parents will be inclined to push for excessive privileges. I've encountered families where the kids want a chartered plane to take them and their friends to spend spring break in Cabo. Or they expected Dad to indulge them in a new sports car when they got their license (or worse, when they hit a midlife crisis and still haven't reached self-sufficiency).

It's only natural that sometimes kids from wealthy families will push the limits to see what monetary requests will or won't fly. If you want your kids to ultimately learn self-respect and independence, these are exactly the times when you'll want to hold the line. Just as you want to refrain from wielding your money as power over your offspring, you want to help them refrain from throwing that weight around as well.

One of the big trademarks of families that keep money is plain old delayed gratification. If something is worth wanting, it's worth waiting for. The only way to foster that life-enriching skill in your heirs is to refrain from running every aspect of their lives, buying everything they want, and solving all their problems.

A LIFELONG EXPECTATION OF INDEPENDENCE

A key caveat of parenting that respects the kids' individuality is that even though you'll be supportive of your children finding their own way and choosing their own priorities, they need to know from the beginning that they must be self-sufficient in the lives they create.

Consider a few families who've successfully pushed money down through generation after generation, like the Rothschilds, the Rockefellers, and some of the royal families of Europe. One of the biggest old-money secrets they share is that they raise their children *from birth* with the expectation that they'll do something meaningful through their own works or sacrifices—whether those are in business, in charitable works, in military service, or in some other way they themselves define. Their children know from the beginning that one day they'll be expected to stand on their own. In the best scenarios, how they choose to do that is up to them.

A HIDDEN UPSIDE OF DITCHING THE MINI-ME MINDSET

Viewing your kids as individuals with their own minds is a matter of mutual affection and respect for the adults they will become (or have become). It's also a matter of letting kids find their own paths—without you pulling the strings or paving the road before them.

Ditching the mini-me mindset has both short-term and long-term rewards, in no small part because when you show your kids you respect them as people, you make it easier for them to view you as "just" a person, too. For kids who grow up with wealthy and powerful parents, this is a big deal. There may be moments when you'd like your kids to recognize all you've accomplished, but most of the time your relationships are better served if they see you as simply Dad or Mom—the person who loves them most and wants the best for them.

THE "HOW" IS UP TO YOU

If you're wondering how to make the shift from steering your kids where you want them to go to setting them free to figure out who they are and how they can be self-supporting, it starts with two simple but potentially challenging attitudes: listening and waiting.

This doesn't mean being entirely hands-off. You're still the parent. Only you can decide where to draw the line on your direct influence. I've seen families successfully navigate this path in many different ways. For example:

- A Midwestern couple I've worked with for decades built and sold a number of businesses to achieve great wealth. They told each of their kids they'd pay their costs to earn a bachelor's degree (and a master's if they wanted to pursue it). The only caveat was a simple one: *By the beginning of sophomore year, you must be able to tell me how you expect to leverage your degree to build a career and become self-supporting.*

- The Florida family that had long planned to bring the kids into the business. When their daughter chose to become an educator and their son chose a career in the arts, the parents didn't pour their energy into steering them back toward the company. Instead, they began working on a long-term plan that would allow the parents to retire, would see the company go into capable hands, and would give them enough financial security to one day set up trust funds for the kids if they chose to do so. They supported their offspring in pursuing their individual career dreams but made it clear the kids would have to be self-sufficient in them.

- The Southwestern family now moving an inherited fortune into their third generation. The second generation learned from an early age that they were expected to work during summer breaks and after college—either in the family business or elsewhere. Now the third-generation kids have been raised with that same expectation—that everybody works, though where is entirely up to them. They, too, are thriving. A notable act of love and respect this family has done is reading and treasuring a series of letters from the grandfather about business principles, personal priorities, and special memories. I'm sure many families have similar letters that've been lost or forgotten in an attic or a basement, but very few spotlight this kind of deeply personal legacy from their elders.

When in doubt about how to handle choices their heirs were making, each of these families defaulted to asking questions instead of dictating answers. They asked the kids what was most important to them, and they asked how they were going to make their choices work in the real world—where budgets and bills are a reality that can't be ignored.

Chapter 3

STRUGGLE:
THE MISSING PIECE

"I just don't want my kids to struggle like I did."

This one sentiment is nearly universal among parents. When the parents have significant wealth, it carries new weight—because money does solve a lot of problems. It can knock down barriers. It can ease transitions. It can influence others to support your objectives.

Even so, when parents come into my office and make this statement, I ask them to consider a different mindset—one in which they may *want* their kids to struggle. Because struggle, when it comes down to it, is the single biggest key to developing feelings of self-worth, purpose, and even happiness. It is the nature of hardship that it builds character and confidence.

Seneca wrote, "No man is more unhappy than he who never faces adversity, for he is never permitted to prove himself."

In the 2,000 years since that statement, it has only become more true. I know you want to support your kids and grandkids. It's important to recognize, though, that sooner or later they *are* going to struggle. In most cases, sooner is better. Most of us are best served by learning lessons early and on a manageable scale than we are learning them late when they're going to change the course of our lives.

Consider what it means to let your kids get out in the world and take their lumps when they're young. Maybe they'll do poorly in a class, or make mistakes at a job, or spend their whole paycheck on concert tickets and be broke until the next one. These lessons about effort, accountability, and frugality are ones most kids, teens, and young adults experience on the road to adulthood. The alternative is quite different, though, in families with the clout of wealth. I'm sure it's well within your power to get overly involved to help with that class, making it your concern whether your child has the best possible tutor (whether they want one or not) or whether the grading is perfectly fair. It's certainly within your reach to offer or secure a job where your kid will carry minimal responsibilities and another employee will be responsible for preventing or cleaning up their mistakes. And you could, if you wanted to, transfer funds to your child or provide a credit card you pay every month in order to ensure they never run out of cash.

In each case, it's a crisis averted. Or is it? Because if your child doesn't get the chance to learn to react, recover, and reset after their mistakes, they're not going to be prepared for the real world—or for dealing with the bigger hurdles life will eventually put before them. Lessons in effort, accountability, and many other basic values have a way of circling back around time and again until a person truly learns them.

A WORKING WORLD

Embracing the spirit of struggle means your kids must do the work themselves. Whether they're in school, in sports, in a job, or in any competitive situation, the only way they gain the knowledge, insight, and confidence they'll need all their lives is to find their own way through.

At Oxbow, we believe the sooner this starts, the better, and we advise families of young people to prepare them for a predetermined finish line for financial support in their youth. For most, this point is at the end of their formal education. I personally believed that part of my responsibility to my children was to allow them to get a college education without debt. I also chose to cover the cost of a sensible car for each of them. Those simple parameters are the same ones I routinely recommend to wealthy parents: pay for an education; and provide a safe car.

And that's it for a long while.

The time to let your kids know this is the way things will go is when they are young. Don't share the limits of your financial support as a threat or a punishment, because that's not what they are. They are an affirmation of your confidence in your kids' ability to invest in themselves—to work and study and try and fail and learn by being in the grind. That is their path to true self-respect, and you have to get the money out of the way for them to be able to take it. If the kids know all along that you love them and believe in them—but are not going to be the source of dollar-sign solutions to real-life problems—they'll be free to get upright on their own.

There's a great book by Greg Lukianoff and Jonathan Haidt called *The Coddling of the American Mind* that takes a deep dive into the damage being done in the service of paranoid parenting and safety-ism. It's been lauded by everyone from Michael Bloomberg to Neil DeGrasse Tyson to Bill Gates for its analysis of parenting and campus trends that stifle independent thinking and action. The main premise Lukianoff and Haidt put forth is that as a society and in our families we must choose to "prepare the child for the road, not the road for the child." That phrase would be a good mantra for any wealthy parent working to raise heirs who will one day develop strength, character, and depth.

Another adage wealthy parents would be wise to take to heart comes from Thomas Edison, who sagely advised, "Opportunity is missed by most people because it is dressed in overalls and looks like work."

HOW LONG?

I often tell investors to set flight to their children and let them be on their own for seven to ten years after college. This is an ideal time for them to truly learn to navigate the road. Give them an education and a decent car and then put away your checkbook. This is not the time for you to buy their houses or to pay for dream vacations or to foot their bills. It's a time for them to face adversity and build character. The older they get, the greater the toll struggle will take, so don't put yourself between the kids and early opportunities to strive.

In many cases, parents take this advice to mean they should hire their kids to work for them. Consider this with some skepticism, and know that hiring the kids right out of school is something we at Oxbow do not advise. Bringing the kids into the company may be a winning endgame if that's what you both want, but in all seriousness, would you hire anybody else who had no experience? And would you trust the gentle training your employees would give your kid to hold up to whatever tough lessons they'd get out in the real world? Even if you set out to avoid favoritism, it's a tough line to hold.

On the other hand, if your kids go get jobs on their own and pour in all the effort it takes to achieve without the family name over the door, then they'll be able to not just make it in your company down the line, but to thrive and ultimately to lead.

If this all sounds like tough love to you, think back to your own situation. How hard did you work to earn what you have? How many times did you fail and learn a lesson that could only come through trial and error? How much determination would you have within you today if you'd had it all handed to you?

The truth is, you faced hardships, you learned, and you are stronger (and likely happier) today because of your struggle.

Seventeenth-century philosopher Immanuel Kant wrote that there were three rules of happiness: "Something to do. Someone to love. Something to look forward to."

It is far too easy for the well-meaning wealthy parent to rob their offspring of one, two, or all three of these essential components of a life well lived. They can take "something to do" off the table by removing the need for self-sufficiency. They can make finding someone to love incredibly difficult by thwarting their kids' chances to build self-esteem. And they can eliminate the joys of having something to look forward to by ensuring their kids wait for nothing. The trouble is this: If you create a situation where there's no effort needed for your heirs to embrace these three components of a full and rewarding life, you may take away the lifeblood of their souls.

Give your kids opportunities to develop confidence through accomplishment, and in the long run, both you and they will be happier for it.

OXBOW NOTE:

Strange as it may sound, holding on to wealth often turns out to be even harder for families than getting it in the first place. The majority of wealthy Americans fail to keep their fortunes in the family for more than a single generation—and many don't make it that far. If you'd like a free copy of our book The Psychology of Staying Rich: How to Preserve Wealth and Establish an Enduring Financial Legacy, *contact us at OxbowAdvisors.com.*

Chapter 4

TEACHING
BY EXAMPLE

General James Mattis once wrote that attitudes are "caught, not taught."

This is wisdom you can put into practice in your own home. If working toward getting your heirs out on their own feels like foregoing valuable opportunities to influence their values and outcomes, think again. It's true that you can't force your priorities, character, desires, or dislikes on your kids. But through their childhood and beyond, you can show them who you are and what's important to you. Whether your example is values-centered and loving, critical and angry, or some other combination of traits, some of it will ultimately be catching.

Never forget that when there's a great divide between what you tell your children and what you show them, they're likely to default to the latter. With that in mind, make a point to self-check what you're teaching the kids about money. It's all too common for parents who've come into significant wealth to go on epic spending sprees and start living lifestyles designed to show the world they've made it. I understand the impulse. In the moment, it may seem like a logical way to make the transition from an old lifestyle to a new one. But be careful about your excesses, because your kids (of all ages) are taking notes.

I'm not suggesting you hide your wealth. This is not about downsizing your house or skipping vacations. You've earned those things. But do take a hard look at the role money plays in your sense of self-esteem. If you're trying to buy importance and respect—deliberately or unknowingly—your kids may well do the same. And since they didn't make the money, they may spend the rest of their lives trying to prove they have the resources to live large. I've seen this in action—in the form of heirs as old as their 40s, 50s, and even 60s tagging along at the patriarch's every event and meeting, trying to look important and pretending to wield the family fortune. Trust me when I say you don't want that life for your kids. It's a sad and insecure existence.

So what do you show them instead?

- *Show quiet confidence.* Show your kids you don't need to prove your wealth to anyone. Don't consume or brag just because you can. If your sense of self-worth doesn't hang on flaunting money, your kids are far less likely to find theirs that way either.

- *Show respect for everyone.* Your kids are constantly internalizing the way you treat them, the way you treat your spouse, and the way you treat your employees, colleagues, and people in the service world. In time, there's a good chance they will mimic your attitudes in some of their own relationships. One of the most effective and easy antidotes to raising kids who reek of privilege and perceived superiority is to show them every day of their young lives that you give the same respect and courtesy to the waiter as you do to the accountant or the CEO, and that behind closed doors you show genuine regard for every member of your family and household.

- *Show gratitude.* No matter how you built your business or gained your wealth, no matter how hard you worked, also acknowledge that fortune, fate, or faith has favored you. Let your kids know you are grateful for all you have. This simplest of key values is one that's easily "inherited" by kids who are around it.

- The gratitude mentality can extend even to otherwise negative scenarios. For example, I often remind advising clients griping about hefty tax bills (even after they've utilized every legal advantage to lower them) that there's an entirely different way to view the situation. The ones who grew up without much know exactly what I'm talking about—that it's only high earners who have to deal with their particular problem. You can choose to count your blessings, or you can choose to bemoan the costs that come with them. Whenever you can, choose the former.

- *Show them money does not equal identity.* "Wealthy" is just one small part of who you are (and by extension who your kids are). Be sure they have regular opportunities to see the other facets of your identity and personality. Show them by your actions that you're honest, or kind, or healthy, or hard working, or generous—or all of these. Also show them that you choose to work on yourself—whether that means working out, eating egg whites, reading, and even just asking questions. It's an eye-opener for kids when they realize the people they think have it all are still growing and learning.

- *Show them philanthropy.* One of the most important lessons you can teach your heirs is that they can use resources to contribute to a greater good. The feeling of using time, energy, or money to lift up another person or group can be transformative—especially for an heir who struggles to make peace with relationship to wealth.

- I often ask my wealthiest clients—people I know for a fact do a tremendous amount of good in their communities—if their kids see their philanthropy and if they're involved in it. For a surprising number of them, the answer is *no*. The point here isn't to virtue signal your way to good kids. It's that your genuine commitment to a greater good can be infectious. As you demonstrate this key value to your kids, help them understand that the point of generosity is *meeting a need*, not getting their name on a building or winning an award or even being perceived as a good person

- When my own kids were growing up, we'd deliver groceries and cash to families in need right before Christmas. We'd get a list of names from the police department, go to the bank, shop, and then show up and anonymously hand each family a box, an envelope, and a sincere wish for a Merry Christmas. I grew up in deep poverty, and it only made sense to me to help where I could in my own community after I had money. At the time, I didn't think much about that natural impulse. But my kids—who are grown and have children of their own now—they remember those trips and those gifts. Those memories helped shape a spirit of philanthropy they share and have carried into their adult lives.

- *Show restraint.* Over the years I've had many clients who could have bought and sold everything in their orbit—but who refrained from doing so for the simple reason that they didn't want their kids to think that's the way the world works. It's not always easy to hold back, and only you can determine where the line is for you and your family, but it's worth asking whether mitigating displays of wealth during your kids' formative years might benefit them in their adult lives.

- *Show ownership.* I often advise parents of teens and young adults—even parents with great wealth—to have their kids fly coach. It's a small gesture that offers a reality check on ownership of the family fortune. The money you have earned is not automatically your kids' money.

  - Now I'm sure your kids are smart. They know if you have a house in Aspen or Hawaii. But they should also know that even if they get to enjoy a family week in those vacation spots in the summer or over the holidays, it doesn't belong to them. They're not going to spend their days lying out by the pool while the rest of their generation is working and finding their place in the world.

Always remember that more of your value system will be passed on by osmosis than by instruction. The kids are watching. Some of my wealthiest and happiest investors still live fairly consistent, normal lifestyles. They could make life a never-ending party for themselves and a cakewalk for their children if they wanted to, but they don't—because that kind of life can squelch a child's highest ambitions.

Chapter 5

HOW AND WHEN TO TALK ABOUT THE MONEY

Whether you're making your first 10 million, working toward 100 million, or investing a billion dollars, work forward on the presumption that there's going to be a fortune at your disposal one day soon—and certainly there will be one at the end of your life. Then ask yourself: What can you do today to ensure that money becomes a boon instead of a burden to your kids?

One thing's for certain: What most people are doing right now is less than ideal. A white paper from The Spectrem Group took a deep dive into baby boomer wealth transfers and found that

37 percent of interviewees *expected* disputes over their estates. That's an abysmal stat, and the discouraging numbers keep coming. The study also found that:

- 52% of adults surveyed don't even have a will.

- 40% of those who received an inheritance felt it was not fair.

- 40% of parents who had wealth said they'd never had estate conversations with their kids.

These numbers are consistent with my experience—with the fact that many, maybe most, families deal with wealth by not talking about it. In the past decade or so, the estate-planning industry has undertaken a massive overcorrection in this area for the wealthiest families, encouraging them to bring the kids in for "family governance" instruction from the time they're teens.

At Oxbow, we're of the mind that neither of these approaches is an effective one. The first—not talking about the wealth—allows confusion, anxiety, and hard feelings to fester in the vacuum it creates. The second—disclosing the family fortune and its management to a kid who's never earned a dime or budgeted anything but an allowance—can be equally disastrous. In many ways, it's like sitting your heirs down and telling them the stakes of their initiatives and actions are and always will be irrelevant. That's a poisonous thought to a young mind.

It's no wonder the failure rate for successful wealth transfer is so high when these all-or-nothing approaches are the most practiced. You have heirs who don't know a thing and heirs who know more than is healthy for them—and neither is prepared to inherit with much wisdom or grace.

With this in mind, let's look at an effective middle road to teaching your kids about money, focusing on both timing and content of key conversations.

FIRST THING'S FIRST

The most important conversations you'll ever have about your financial and family legacy are the ones you'll have without the kids. Sit down with your spouse and talk about your priorities and desires. Get things straight between you. Then meet together with your estate lawyer, and get things straight there, too. It's critical to the longevity of the wealth you pass on to the next generation that you are in agreement about what's most important to you and how your estate plans will help make it happen. Far too many estate plans start falling apart the minute one parent dies, because it turns out Mom and Dad never put their heads together and came to an agreement on how and when they'd move money to the kids.

There are many effective tools for moving wealth between generations, and I encourage you to explore them with a trusted advisor (you'll also read about some broadly valuable approaches in the next chapter). It's important to note, though, that in their determination to manage the mechanisms, many families forget that the biggest ingredient of wealth-transfer success is the way you raise the kids—an area where effective communication is key. No matter how you do the estate plan, if you haven't fostered them in finding independence and fortitude, little else will matter. They'll find a way to blow it, or they'll find a way to tear the family apart with it, or both.

FIRST TOPICS

Among the earliest conversations about wealth you'll want to have with your kids are the ones about how hard it can be to earn a wage. The jobs and eventual careers they'll have will teach them this in time, but if they're living in a big house in a posh neighborhood with a tennis club and a full fridge, the sooner they understand that most of the world gets by paycheck to paycheck, the better. Set a course for a sense of financial responsibility by letting your kids find out how hard it can be earned with a day's work.

After the value of work, the concept of a budget should not be far behind. As Morgan Housel, author of the bestselling *The Psychology of Money*, wrote in an open letter to his newborn daughter, "The person who makes $50,000 but only needs $40,000 to be happy is richer than the person who makes $150,000 but needs $151,000 . . . The investor who earns a 5% return with low expenses may be better off than the investor who earns 7% a year and needs every penny."

Learning that there are many people in this world who will never have "enough" should be a key part of a young person's financial education.

Another topic that can start as early as the first lemonade stand and continue throughout life is the value of entrepreneurship. Encourage entrepreneurial spirit without writing blank checks, and encourage your kids to look at problems with the intention of finding solutions on their own. Doing so may require you to take a step back and wait while they think and test their theories, but getting comfortable with that process will serve them well all their lives.

ONE KEY INVESTMENT PRINCIPLE

No matter how we investigate or parse the financial outcomes of wealthy families working to move wealth between generations, one guideline can set a firm foundation for nearly any scenario. It's the same recommendation I give to every entrepreneur who's sold a business, every athlete who's landed a once-in-a-lifetime contract, and every heir who comes into substantial wealth: *Learn and respect the difference between base capital and investment capital.*

If you are in possession of substantial wealth, you owe it to yourself and to your heirs to make this distinction and to ensure they know it as well. The crux of it is this: A portion of your family's fortune exists to provide a security net and a reliable income. That's your base capital. It is not to be gambled, staked, or spent. It serves as a net under every other investment and financial decision you make—during your lifetime and, ideally, after it. When your kids are old enough to talk about investment strategy, this is where their education should start.

Safeguarding base capital is key to effective inheritance strategies on both psychological and practical levels. When you rely on base capital in your own budget, it is the portion of your portfolio that covers your living expenses, insurance, medical expenses, and other expected costs of living. Depending on your level of wealth and number of heirs, you may ultimately be able to pass on that same level of security. Or perhaps, like many families who successfully move money from generation to generation, you can designate the income from your base capital to be set aside for educational costs, wedding gifts, down payments, or other life-milestone expenses. Heirs who understand that a portion of the family's riches are and will remain in a metaphorical vault also understand one of the most important tenets of wealth: that if you have it, you should never lose it.

ONE-ON-ONE CONVERSATIONS

Many parents misconstrue advice to treat their children equally (see Chapter 8) to mean they should address money matters with them as a group. This is not your best tack for a couple of reasons. First, each of your heirs will benefit from having a chance to speak with just you and your spouse about family money. This gives them the freedom to ask questions and share their feelings without being under the scrutiny of their siblings. Second, an individual approach gives you the ability to tailor each conversation to your child's age, needs, personality, and objectives.

This isn't a one-and-done situation. It's not like the sex talk where once you've explained the basics they're informed for life. Conversations about family wealth should be ongoing and age appropriate. In the early years, this means shielding your kids from numbers for which they have no perspective. The company may be worth $50 million, for example, but to a young adult that just sounds like a mountain of cash. To you, it's likely the culmination of decades of work, sacrifice, and strategy—and it's earmarked for decades of security for you and yours.

This disconnect between the way the wealth earner views the family fortune and the way the kids likely see it is the key problem with popular "governance" approaches to legacy planning. So many firms want to bring the kids in early, maybe at 14 or 15 or 18, and teach them about the family wealth. I couldn't disagree more with this method. The kids are too immature. They haven't worked. Why do they need to know about the money? If you want to eventually transfer your fortune to people who are humble, who work hard, and who appreciate what they have, you must wait until they get a sense of what money means in the real world. Besides, why would you ever choose to thwart their ambition early by telling them, in effect, that money will never be an object? You're far better off to let them get out there and start climbing life's ladder with a hunger for success.

THE DREADED TALK

The time will come when it is both appropriate and advisable to share some details of your estate plan with the kids. Ideally, the timetable of your life has room for this conversation to wait until the kids have a chance to get an education and find their way into the workforce. This is another reason you and your spouse need to be on the same page—if something happens to one of you, the other should be able to move forward with the same plan you put in place together.

These, too, are individual conversations, not family meetings, and the key thrust of these conversations should be that it is your intention to treat your kids equally in the will.

I have lost count of how many full-grown and self-sufficient adults I've met with—many of them with kids and even grandkids of their own—who tell me they have no idea what's in their parents' will. Don't be one of the parents who keeps the financial future of the family shrouded. You don't need to break out the spreadsheets or get into the fine print, but let them in on your thought process, share your philosophy on philanthropy, your highest priorities, and who you trust to help manage the family wealth.

In truth, once your kids prove they are self-supporting and self-assured, there are many tools you can use to start sharing the family wealth and advising them on your priorities for it long before you leave them. In the next chapter, we'll talk more about living bequests and how they can benefit your estate plan.

OXBOW NOTE:

In my book Your Money Mentality: How You Feel About Risk, Losses, and Gains, *I explain that investing is not linear and that successful investment strategy must sometimes go against conventional wisdom. I walk investors through the highs and lows of the market to help them determine their individual money mentality. If you'd like a complimentary copy of this book, contact us at OxbowAdvisors.com.*

Chapter 6

TIMING, TOOLS, AND A SELF-CHECK FORMULA

A great deal of time and attention in estate planning is dedicated to the tools of transfer: trusts, investments, insurance, annuities, gifts, salaries, and so on. Tools are important, but in the end, it's unlikely they will make or break the peaceful transfer of wealth to your next generation. Instead, if problems arise, they'll be the attitudes and relationships in the family that matter most.

A 2024 Bank of America/Escalent survey of wealthy families found that inheritance-related strains are attributed to, in order of prevalence:

- interpersonal family dynamics (a whopping 59%)

- unequal distribution of assets (38%)

- lack of clear instructions (25%)

- lack of communication (24%)

These aren't failures of the plans. They are failures of the people. If you are committed to seeing the wealth you've earned kept in your family, the mechanisms by which you prepare the money for the kids are the smallest part of the work ahead. More important by far is how you prepare the kids for the money.

The first rule of making financial gifts work is *don't give vast sums of money to half-formed people.* There's an old adage in Hollywood that a star stops maturing at the age when they become famous. The same can be said for taking control of significant wealth. When you can simply buy anything you want, and when people defer to you wherever you go, it gets extremely difficult to remain ambitious and committed to personal or professional growth. It also gets really hard to tell who your true friends are and who is just hanging around to be near the money.

The trick, then, becomes figuring out the right time and the right amounts to help your heirs without curbing their drive, sense of independence, and all-important self-esteem.

First, let's consider a few guidelines for the timing of financial gifts:

- *Don't give too soon.* Your 18-year-old doesn't need a Ferrari, a condo in Palm Beach, or half a million dollars in the bank. Thousands of wealthy families can attest to the pitfalls of showering young heirs with money at the time when they are most in need of opportunities to learn and mature. Let the kids grow and prove (to themselves even more than to you) that they can handle the pressures of life before bestowing the mixed blessings of wealth.

- *Don't impede independence.* This may sound like a trick answer to a parent who's in a position to simply gift financial independence. But in truth, the line you don't want to cross isn't a dollar figure but rather a will to succeed. What level of support from you would keep your kids from going after their own salary and living on it? You want to stay on the right side of that equation. The earlier you start setting this parameter, the better, because a worst-case scenario is one in which you give too much, too early, and then somewhere down the line you realize the kids are too dependent and have to pull back. When that happens, resentments abound. If you never set up the expectation that you'll be funneling money to your young heirs at a significant level, then you'll never have to face that particular crisis.

- *Don't feel the need to go all-in.* Inheritance doesn't have to be an all-or-nothing proposition. In fact, it's likely best if it is not. Some of the best financial legacy plans I've seen share funds with the kids at staggered intervals. The kids get to "practice" on smaller sums and it helps prepare them for long-term legacy.

- *Don't wait too long.* Almost worse than situations where the kids have been given too much, too soon, are the ones where they're still subservient to their parents, waiting to be financially independent, into their 40s, 50s, and later. By the time your offspring are in their mid-30s, you should be able to tell if they're on the road to long-term confidence and self-sufficiency. At that point, you can comfortably consider using gifts or trusts to give them access to a portion of the assets you envision one day passing down. Doing so has a number of benefits—providing funds at a time when your kids are settling into their adult lives, allowing you to offer those gifts while you're still around to answer questions about them, and creating real trials in which the kids can learn important investment lessons without squandering your life's savings. Most importantly, *not* giving a portion of your accumulated wealth to your kids at this later life stage can create terrible bitterness. I've met heirs who are angry and who are basically waiting for their parents to die before they take ownership of their lives. It's an ugly dynamic, one to be avoided at all costs.

- *Turn to trusts.* Every billionaire I've ever interviewed has told me the same thing with regard to ensuring financial security for future generations: that they will manage the flow of wealth through trusts. These tools are so varied and complex that they warrant a book of their own—and an advising expert to walk you through your unique needs and options. Regardless of what form of trust you choose or how you structure it, though, consider including some mechanism that's partly controlled by a third party—a corporate executor who will work in tandem with your heirs or the individual you choose to represent your interests. This takes some of the weight and emotional baggage off the kids and puts it on the shoulders of an entity built to hold it.

  - In decades of financial advising and collaborating with estate attorneys, I've seen a majority of estate plans that simply default to the oldest son to fulfill the trustee role. This is a disservice to women, to younger children who've proven they have their heads on straight, and—most importantly—to the relationships between your kids. In concert with your spouse and advisor, consider which, if any, of your children is best able to fulfill this role—or whether they are capable of working together on it. The question isn't who was born first or who you like best, but rather who is most able to do the job without it taking a huge emotional toll.

Once you've made these decisions, sit down with your heirs—individually—and talk about your expectations.

A MOVEABLE PLAN

Decades ago, Warren Buffett made the oft-quoted comment that he planned to give his children enough money that they could do anything, but not enough that they could do nothing. It was excellent advice. As time passed, however, Buffett changed his mind. He realized his kids had grown up to be wise, capable adults, and that they could handle more. Today, all three are philanthropists working to effectively deploy the family fortune to causes around the world.

You should always have a plan in place in order to avoid family chaos if something happens to you. But your plan should evolve along with your relationships and your kids' maturity. Take a little time each year to assess where things stand and what is most important to you, and adjust your plans accordingly.

TOOLS

Tools for wealth transfers abound, and every family's needs are a bit different from those of the next. A reputable financial advisor can help you structure gifts, trusts, and bequests that maximize the security of your estate and its tax efficiency. The purpose of this book isn't to lay out the nuts and bolts of inheritance structure, but rather to help you prepare the next generation of your family to handle that inheritance when it comes their way. With that in mind, consider these tools you can use to teach your heirs how to manage wealth:

- *Limited gifts.* When your child demonstrates they can hold a job and be self-sufficient, that's a good time to see how they manage a cash inflow. US tax code allows parents to transfer a tax-excluded gift to each child, each year. At this writing, that figure is $19,000, and the cap typically goes up every year. If you're reading this book, odds are $19,000 makes no dent in your net worth, but if you've pushed your kids out of the nest and seen them learn to earn and budget, it'll probably make a significant impact on theirs. This kind of small-windfall gift gives your heirs the opportunity to save, spend, invest, or pay down debt—all without jeopardizing their future inheritance or your bottom line. The purpose of giving this gift isn't to control the way the money is spent (which would make it not a gift at all). It's to observe how your heirs handle the money and if they're comfortable, confident, and mindful with it.

- *Investment accounts.* As your heirs come into their own in adulthood, you're going to want them to learn the basics of risk tolerance, balanced investment, and working with trusted professionals to protect their base capital and grow their investments. With this in mind, you can gift a non-consumable account for your child to manage. As with any early financial gift, the point of this exercise is not to transfer substantial wealth. Instead, it's to teach an understanding and respect of investment principles. By setting up an account with your seed money, you give your child a chance to see their choices play out in real time. Don't judge them harshly on whether they earn or lose. In this short-term scenario, that's not the most important outcome. What matters most is whether your heir takes the role seriously, whether they're able to collaborate with and listen to an advisor, and whether they're able to better appreciate that family wealth isn't for spending—it's for generating income (an income you may eventually allow them to spend or reinvest).

- *Hands-on practice.* One of the more valuable exercises I've seen families with long-term financial legacies employ is supporting (but not bankrolling) an adult heir's desire to go into business. Among those scenarios, the most instructive may be the purchase of an investment property. In this circumstance, a parent may co-sign on a loan for the heir or lend them a down payment to get into a small-scale real estate investment—perhaps a modest commercial property. The key here is to have the child do the work. They need to find a property, build a business plan, visit the bank for financing, set up the insurance, manage the lease and maintenance, and oversee the relevant accounts and repayment plan. This is a significant step up in the learning department from a simple cash gift, and in my experience, it is one of the most instructive experiences an heir with a mind to be in your business (or any business) can undertake. It's a microcosm of the bigger financial world and a great way for a motivated young person to learn in a hands-on way.

- *Partial inheritance.* If your adult heir is self-supporting and handles any one of these first-step transition tools in a way that makes you comfortable with giving more, you may consider gifting them an incrementally bigger sum. The benefits of doing so during your lifetime are many. Your heirs may have young families and be looking to buy first or bigger houses. They may want to start college accounts for their kids. They may have investment dreams. Whatever you give during this time, make sure your family knows you stand ready to offer advice based on a lifetime of experience and successful wealth building. Some will ask for guidance, and some won't, but giving them access to your insights is one of the biggest benefits of giving away money while you're still alive.

· These gifts must never impinge on your ability to meet all of your own financial needs for the rest of your life. That is your highest priority. Over the years, it has been shocking and discouraging to me how many first-generation wealth creators are willing to risk their own financial well-being for those of kids who are still in the workforce (or who should be). Don't let yourself fall into their ranks.

• *Philanthropic role.* Another financial training tool is establishing a fund or a budget your heirs may use to benefit a philanthropic entity. This should be more than a cash-in/cash-out situation. Have the kids do their homework, understand the budget of the recipient, and know how their donations will be spent. This one-step-removed assessment of business plans and budgets can provide valuable insights and experience, as well as inspiration to lead a philanthropic life.

In every gifting scenario, I advise you to offer whatever you intend to share without strings. You can offer guidance, but don't use the money to hold onto control. This is another reason to not start with a huge windfall. I've seen heirs blow the whole thing within a year or two and then come back looking for a piece of the parents' base capital. The answer to this request must always be a resounding *no*.

SELF-CHECK FORMULA

If you're not sure whether you're doing too much for your heirs before they're ready, there's a simple way to self-assess. Consider what percentage of their expenses you're covering. 10 percent? 50 percent? Everything but groceries? If you're paying most life costs for your young adult kids, you're not doing them any favors. Every family is different, but I recommend keeping your contributions below 20 or 25 percent. Another way to approach this test is to ask yourself, whatever your number is: If you stopped paying, could they make it? If the answer is *no*, then you're doing a disservice to your children and your future grandchildren as well.

There's a reason families that are most successful in passing down money don't just drop a windfall on their heirs when they turn 18 or 21 or 25. Many have structured gifts so future generations receive a small gift after graduation and the cost of an education. Not until later in life do those heirs come into life-changing sums of money—not until after they've proven (more to themselves than to you) that they are capable of surviving on their own. Once that happens, you can confidently gift more without worrying you'll spoil their confidence or ambition.

Chapter 7

IN-LAWS AND EXTENDED FAMILY

The X factor most families don't sufficiently consider in estate planning is the people who will come into the picture from outside your inner circle. Your kids will likely have spouses, in-laws, and other extended family members. With half of marriages ending in divorce, you can't afford not to think about how these new players and close relationships might impact your estate plans.

WHAT TO DO

One of the advantages of allowing the teens and young adults in your family to struggle and become self-sufficient early in their careers is that the process of exploring who they are and what they're capable of will give them a healthy sense of self-esteem. Some of the most disturbing cases of lost fortunes I've seen were in families where an insecure heir chooses a partner because that person fawns over them, or helps them rebel against their parents, or controls their every move. These are all nightmare situations, and the best way to steer your family clear of them is to let your kids develop the confidence to recognize manipulators and reject them out of hand.

The other meaningful tools at your disposal are your own relationships and what you teach about the nature of romantic and family ties. Your kids are watching the way you interact with your spouse (and with your exes, if that's a factor). If you treat your partner with respect and encourage them to be independent and fulfilled, your kids are going to absorb some of that attitude. On the other hand, if you're secretive, dismissive, or disrespectful, those attitudes may bubble up one day in the kids' relationships. In addition: Teach and show your kids from a young age that a marriage is more than a romance; it is a partnership. True partners share values and goals. They work toward the same outcomes— among them staying close to one another, sharing a happy home, raising children who feel loved and capable, and achieving and maintaining financial security. Show your kids that a marriage is more than hearts and flowers, and you'll be encouraging them to look for deeper qualities in the dating pool than just attractiveness and flattery.

Find the balance between being hospitable and guarded in family and financial matters. It is a tall order to ask wealthy parents to get ready to welcome boyfriends, girlfriends, sons- and daughters-in-law, but it's a necessary one. You don't want to alienate your kids by snubbing their partners, even if (or especially if) there's a good chance that one of them is going to end up in divorce. Be kind, but also be prepared. How do your plans account for family changes? Take time to talk with a trusted financial advisor about scenarios and tools with which an inheritance stays with your children and grandchildren rather than somebody's ex. This is also a time to hold the line on individual conversations about estate plans and family wealth with each of your kids. The day may come when both you and your child want to invite a spouse into those dialogues, but it's okay to go slow in getting there.

Keep lines of communication open. Years ago I worked with a family that inherited an oil and gas fortune of just shy of $100 million. The parents were married for nearly 40 years, and they raised four children together. The Mom was the glue in that family. She handled all the communication—between the parents and the kids and amongst the kids. She kept the peace, and she was good at it. Sadly, when she got sick and passed away in her early 60s, the family went off the rails. Fighting about the money and the property and who Mom loved most began almost immediately. One of the kids still talks to me. None of them speak to each other. The father, inexperienced at communicating with his own children, didn't really even try. He moved on pretty quick and rarely sees the family.

Theirs was a family torn apart by wealth, and they are a cautionary tale for others who could face the same kind of crisis. Run your family in such a way that each person knows they can openly communicate with the others. Have some fun together. Have meaningful conversations. Deal with conflicts and resentments with patience and understanding. Not all heartbreak is avoidable, but a lot of it can be averted when people just know how to talk with one another and are confident that their family members have genuine goodwill for them.

THE THIRD GENERATION AND BEYOND

Far too many first-generation wealth earners fail to look beyond their own children when they create their estate plans. The results can be disastrous. If one member of the second generation passes away early, for example, is there any provision for their spouse or kids? If one sibling spends every dime that comes his way, does that mean your grandchildren may not be able to afford to go to good schools or have any measure of financial security from your estate? And what of divorces and remarriages and all the complications that come with them?

Rather than leave what happens to your wealth in the third generation to fate, consider your options now and make provisions for as many contingencies as you can. Whenever possible, make sure your legacy isn't just in dollars and cents. I'm always amazed when a young person who just inherited a fortune comes to talk with me about investments and they have no idea how the family money was made. As we discussed in Chapter 1, money is only one part of your legacy. The other piece is helping future generations know you and know something of your life, business, and values. Your grandchildren will come into the world in the unique position of never knowing what it's like to *not* have wealth, and you'll face challenges in setting them up to be successful with it. With this in mind, it will fall to you and your children to show Gen Three that as effortless as a life of wealth may look at first glance, tremendous focus, effort, and restraint went into creating it and will continue to be required to maintain it.

Chapter 8

THE ONE RULE
(EQUAL ALL THE WAY)

No matter how you approach decisions about sharing wealth with your family, there is one tenet I advise every parent to stick by, and that is to treat all of your children equally. Failing to do so is the quickest way I know to ruin holidays and family dinners for your kids for the rest of their lives.

If some extenuating circumstance comes up that you feel warrants unequal disbursements of wealth in your lifetime, talk with your kids about it (individually rather than as a group) and explain that in the long run, you will ensure it all evens out in the will. Let them know you love and value them equally and as individuals.

The ways this can play out are as varied as families themselves, but here's a common scenario and how one family made it work:

A family in Oklahoma sold their business for about $60 million while the kids were in college. Mom and Dad retired, invested most of the money, and continued to encourage their kids while both finished school and started their respective careers. Those careers had little in common. One of the kids became a teacher making about $60,000 each year. The other eventually became a doctor making close to $400,000. On the surface, this might have been a challenging situation for the parents. They wanted everything to be equal, but the kids' circumstances were not nearly the same.

What would you do?

There are a lot of right answers, and this family had one of them. First, they changed nothing in their family life or their relationships with their kids during the first years after they sold the company. The kids kept going to school. The parents paid tuition, room, and board for five years for each of them, and after that expected their offspring to contribute with loans or earnings. After school, each of the children did interviews, got a job, got an apartment, and started living an independent life. They came home sometimes for Sunday dinners and for most Thanksgivings, and they all went on occasional vacations as a family. The parents encouraged their kids in their career choices and gave them good advice when they dealt with challenges.

Where was the money during this time? Most of it was tucked

away earning a solid return. Mom and Dad took some great vacations. They did a dream remodel of their kitchen, and they bought a cabin on a lake. They made annual donations to charities that were important to them. They stayed together (though a lot of couples don't when the windfall comes). They toasted their success with some excellent champagne. They were relieved of any burden of ever worrying about money again, and that felt great.

What they did not do was drop millions on a private jet and mansions on both coasts. They did not set up meetings for the kids with their financial advisors to talk about the huge estate they'd one day inherit. They did not change who they were or what was most important to them.

At the 10-year mark, the kids were established in their jobs and their relationships. The parents wrote substantial checks to cover the costs of their weddings, and they were happy to do it. By this time the disparity in their kids' income was more obvious. The teacher was still in an apartment; the doctor had a house in a great neighborhood. And so the parents had individual, private conversations with each child. They offered to cover the down payment on a first house for the teacher, and that child accepted. They offered the same amount of money to pay off med school loans for the doctor, and that was accepted as well. The parents let both kids know this assistance was a one-time gift, and that the gifts were equal. The kids were happy. The parents were happy.

During all this time, most of the money was invested and

growing. By the time the parents sat down with the kids to let them know they'd be receiving a portion of their inheritance to do with what they wanted, the heirs (now approaching 40) were well established in their careers and their lives.

The bulk of the remaining money was put into trusts that could easily generate enough income to provide financial security for the family for generations to come.

It's not a very exciting story—and that is exactly the point. This is the story of a normal family that just happens to have a lot of money. It's not a story *about* the money. If you can, by whatever means works for you, keep the emphasis of your lives on the people and the relationships, you'll all be fine in the long-term transfer of wealth between generations.

Time and again I am reminded of just how important the parents' role is—not just in creating or transferring wealth, but in fostering peace and harmony in the family while they are alive. Doing so gives your children their best possible shot at keeping that peace, their strong relationships, *and* the money after you're gone.

Conclusion

WEALTHY PARENTS, WEALTHY CHILDREN. MAYBE.

There's one more thing we need to talk about—one I'd be remiss to ignore. In truth, parents with wealth often feel that with all the resources at their disposal they should be able to raise perfect kids. They set high standards. Just like everybody else, they love their children and would do anything for them. But sometimes kids from wealthy families—just like kids from across every social stratum—grow up to be irresponsible, or lazy, or dishonest, or drawn to drugs, thrills, or bad relationships. You want better for your kids. You can create the right environment, set the right expectations, and encourage positive behaviors and attitudes. You can choose to give them every opportunity to get their feet under them and grow in confidence.

But then you have to let them choose who they become.

I meet a lot of parents who feel guilty because they weren't around to hands-on parent as much as they would have liked. It makes sense when you think about where the wealth comes from. Most first-generation fortunes are amassed by people who've built one or more businesses and sold them. It's common that during the years they were making that happen, one or both parents worked long days, nights, and weekends. It's entirely possible they didn't always have time to go to the soccer game or help with the math homework or sit down for dinner at 6:00.

When their kids start growing up and making the kinds of mistakes most teens and young adults make, some of these same parents may blame themselves. I see this dynamic all the time, and I see parents who start dishing out money to ease their feelings of worry and remorse.

I tell these parents it's important that they get straight on this—both for their own sake and for that of the kids. Their tales are rarely stories of neglect. They are stories of sacrifice. Most of these parents gave all that time and energy to the company not in spite of their families, but for their families. If this rings familiar to you, it's time to stop beating yourself up. And it's time to stop thinking about buying anybody's forgiveness. There is always a price you pay for success, and if you didn't give quite enough time to your kids when they were growing up to create the legacy you want to share with them in the long run, it's time to let the past go and focus on today.

Instead of worrying about how you're going to make up some perceived failing to the kids, let them know you love them and believe in them. Tell them you want to see them independent and strong and healthy. Be consistent in these truths, and then know that what happens next is up to the kids. That's the hardest part.

The truth is, matters of estates are always complicated—especially when there are great fortunes involved. You've got kids who are different from each other and different from you. There are outside influences on every family. You can't control every factor, but if you follow the guidelines in these chapters, you'll be doing everything in your power to set up a healthy transfer of wealth and positive outcomes for your children and grandchildren.

Wishing continued prosperity for you and yours,
Ted

ABOUT THE AUTHOR

J. TED OAKLEY, founder and managing partner of Oxbow Advisors, has been an investment industry expert for over four decades. The Oxbow Principles and the firm's proprietary investment strategies are founded on the unique perspective he's gained during his long tenure advising high-net-worth investors. Ted's investment advice provides principled guidance to investors from more than half the states in the US. He frequently counsels former business owners on protecting and wisely investing their newly liquid wealth. Ted is the author of several other books, including:

Stay Rich with a Balanced Portfolio: The Price You Pay for Peace of Mind

Your Money Mentality: How You Feel About Risk, Losses, and Gains

You Sold Your Company: Get Ready for Change

$30 Million and Broke: If You Have It, Don't Lose It

The Psychology of Staying Rich: How to Preserve Wealth and Establish an Enduring Financial Legacy

Danger Time: The Two-Year Red Zone After Selling Your Company

Rich Kids, Broke Kids: The Failure of Traditional Estate Planning

Crazy Time: Surviving the First 12 Months After Selling Your Company

My Story: From Poor Kid to Business Owner

Wall Street Lies: 5 Myths to Keep Your Cash in Their Game, with Pat Swanson and Trey Crain